GREAT
MAN
SEEK
GOD
FIRST
E
S
W
N

First edition: 2021

HE BUILDS HIS HOUSE
ON A
SOLID GROUND

CLING
TO YOUR
FAITH
AND KEEP YOUR
CONSCIENCE
CLEAR

STAND
FIRM
ON YOUR
GROUND

A MAN
TESTED
IS A
MAN
THAT CAN BE
TRUSTED

NO temptation
HAS
OVERTAKEN
YOU THAT IS
UNCOMMON
to MAN

AS FOR ME
AND MY
HOUSEHOLD
WE WILL
SERVE
THE LORD

MAN of
GOD
HONORS
HIS
WORDS
PROVERBS

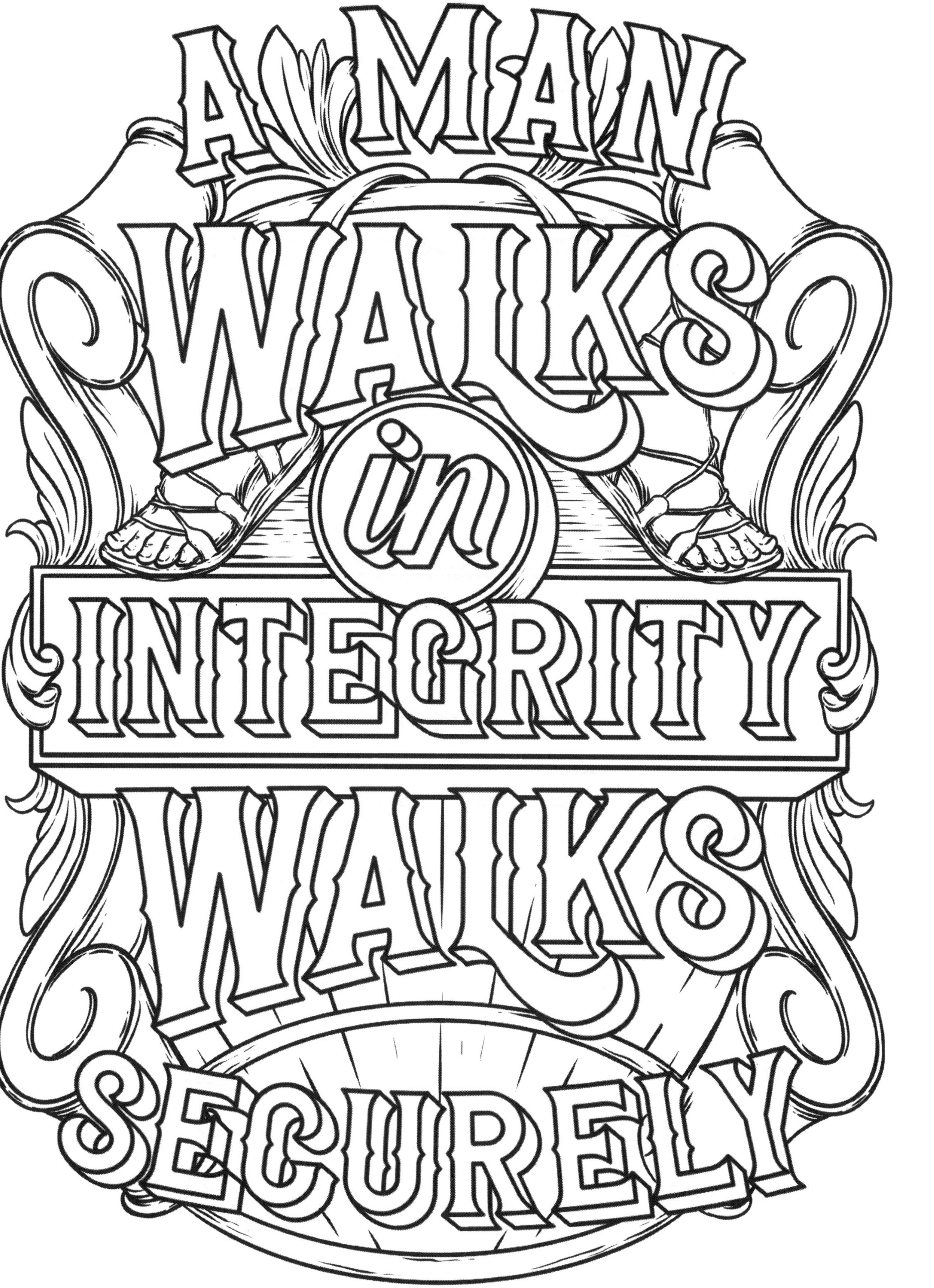
A MAN
WALKS
in
INTEGRITY
WALKS
SECURELY

MAN LOOKS
ON THE
OUTSIDE
APPERANCE
BUT THE
LORD LOOKS
ON THE
HEART

MY
MASCULINITY
IS FOUND IN
HIS
MAJESTY

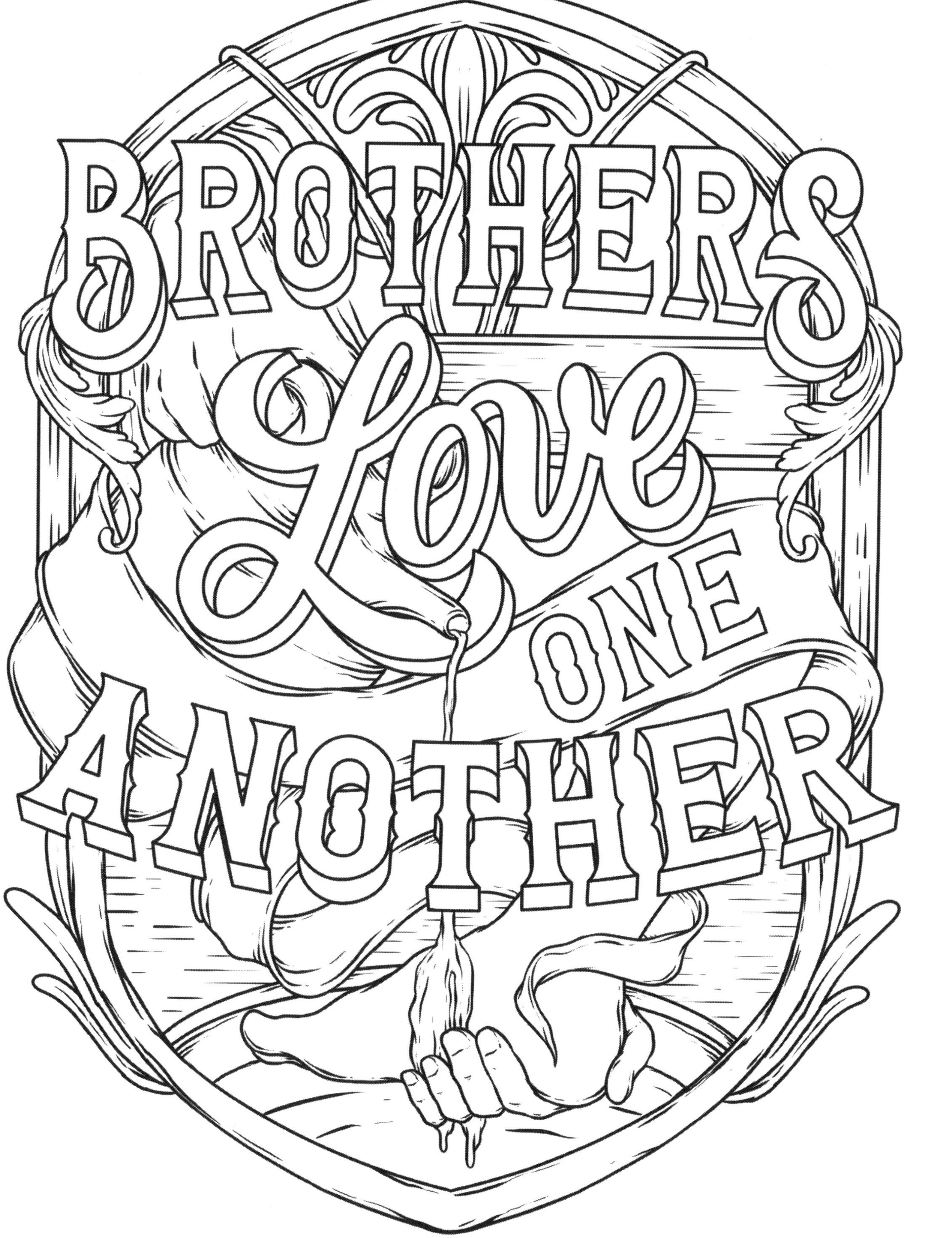
BROTHERS
Love
ONE
ANOTHER

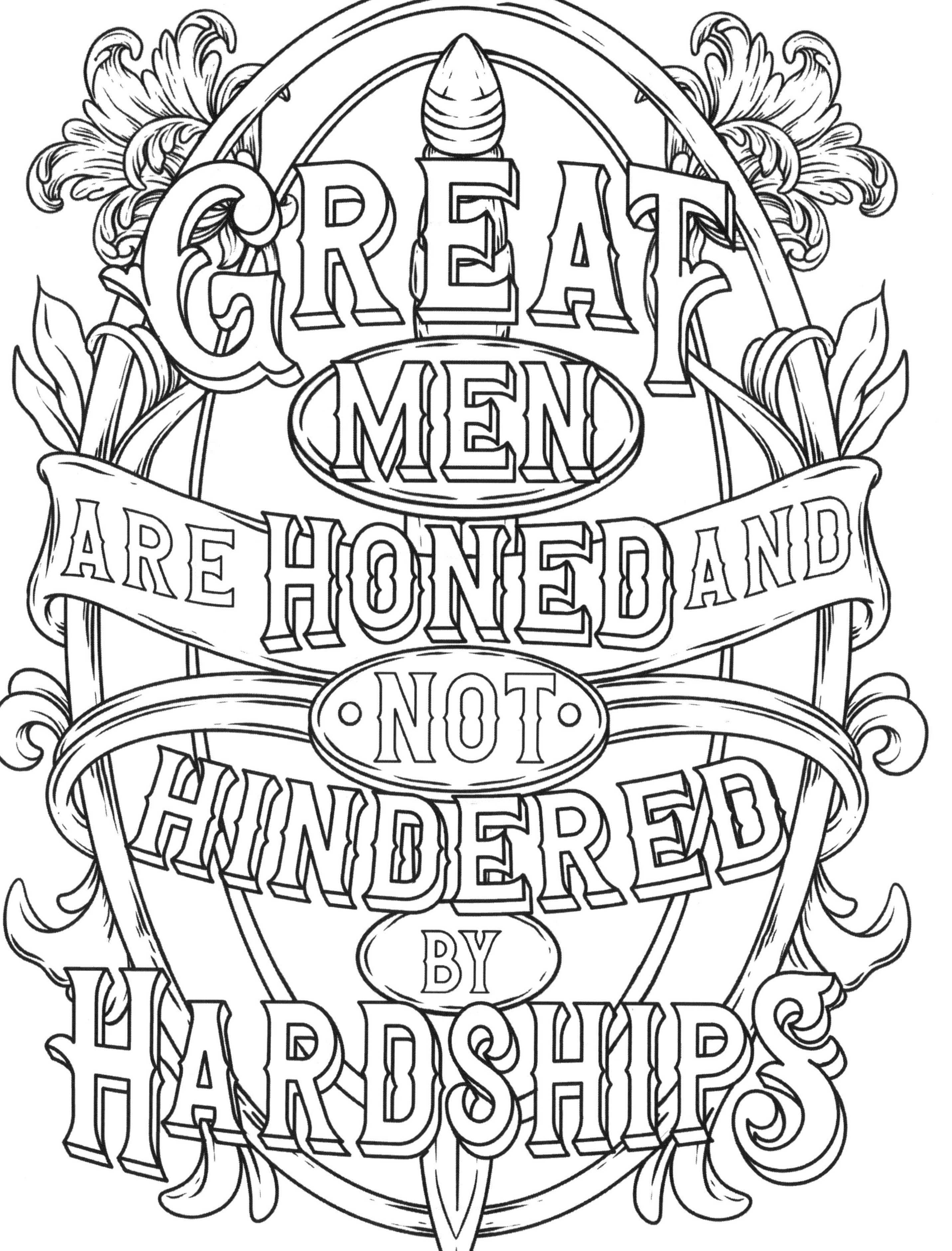
GREAT
MEN
ARE HONED AND
NOT
HINDERED
BY
HARDSHIPS

A MAN OF
UNDERSTANDING
DELIGHTS
IN
WISDOM

A MAN
AFTER
GOD'S
OWN
HEART

WORK HARD
SO YOU CAN
PRESENT
YOURSELF
TO
GOD

A FAITHFUL
MAN
ALWAYS
PROVIDE
FOR HIS
FAMILY

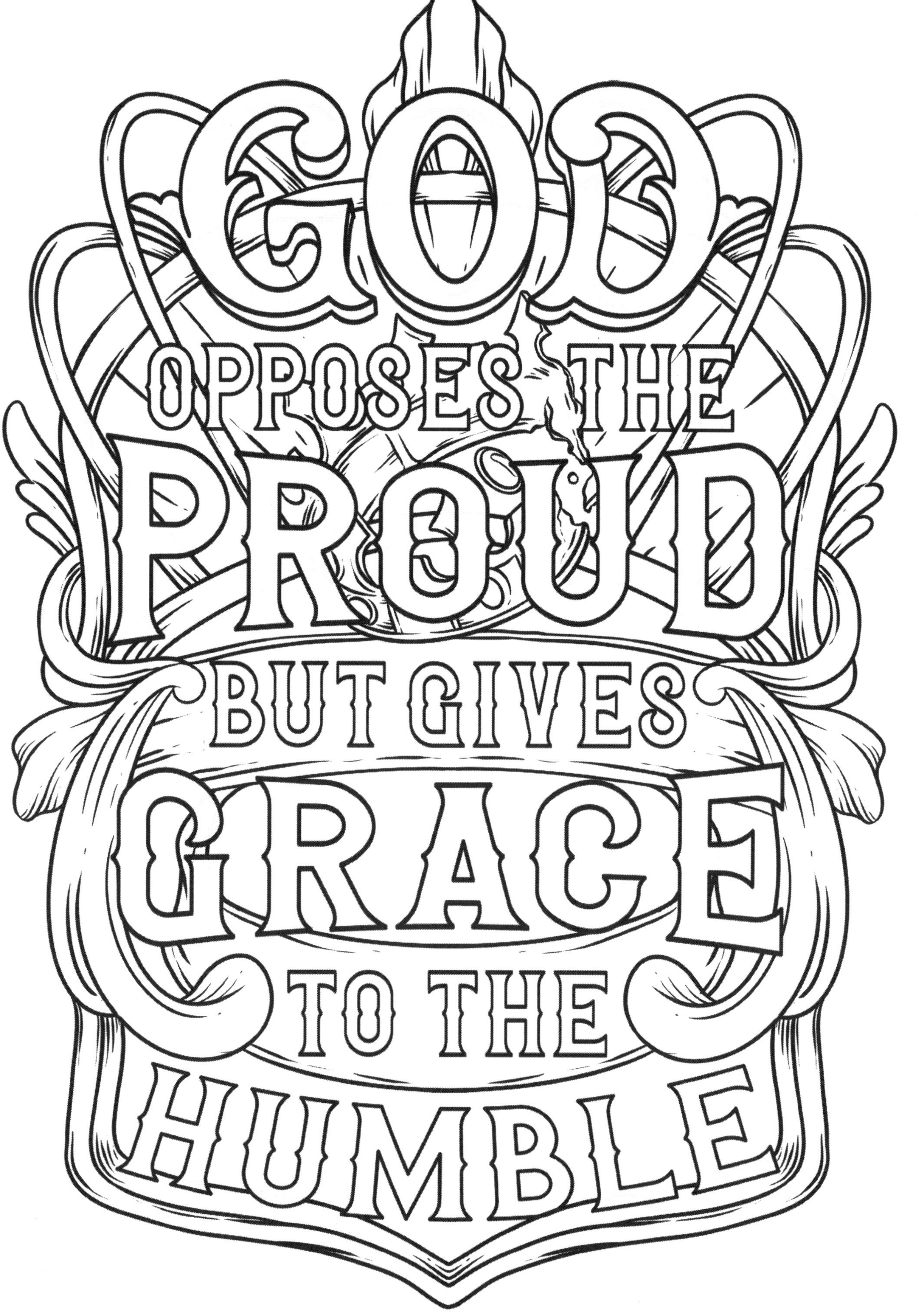
GOD
OPPOSES THE
PROUD
BUT GIVES
GRACE
TO THE
HUMBLE

A RIGHTEOUS
MAN
FALLS
SEVEN TIMES
AND RISES
AGAIN

MAN
MAKES HIS
PLANS
BUT THE LORD
DIRECTS HIS
STEPS

MAN OF GOD
IS ALWAYS
EQUIPPED
FOR EVERY
GOOD
WORKS

REAL MAN
FIGHTS
WITH HIS
KNEES
NOT HIS FIST

HE WHO IS
FAITHFUL
IN LITTLE IS
ALSO FAITHFUL
IN MUCH

GOOD
WORKMANSHIP
STARTS
WITH
GENUINE
WORSHIP

WHATEVER
YOU DO
DO IT
HEARTILY
FOR THE LORD

Made in the USA
Middletown, DE
11 December 2024

66767704R00029